2-15-77

THE MILFORD SERIES

Popular Writers of Today

VOLUME TWO

Alistair MacLean
The Key Is Fear

Robert A. Lee

R. REGINALD
THE Borgo Press
SAN BERNARDINO, CALIFORNIA
MCMLXXVI

Library of Congress Cataloging in Publication Data

Lee, Robert A
Alistair MacLean: the key is fear.

(Popular writers of today; v.2) (The Milford series)
1. MacLean, Alistair, 1922- or 3- — Criticism and interpretation.
PR6063.A248Z75 823'.9'14 76-29047
ISBN 0-89370-203-X

R. Reginald, The Borgo Press is a wholly-owned subsidiary of Lynwyck Realty and Investment Company, Inc., P.O. Box 2845, San Bernardino, CA 92406

First Printing — October, 1976
1 2 3 4 5 6 7 8 9 10

INTRODUCTION

Alistair MacLean is generally regarded as the premier writer of adventure and suspense fiction in the world today. His twenty-one novels range from the American West of the nineteenth century, to World War II, to the espionage games of the Cold War. At his best, he is unmatched in his ability to create believable situations of fear, tension, and terror, and even his mediocre works are better than most suspense novels being marketed today. MacLean makes his magic by the skillful juxtaposition of natural and human threats, the careful unravelling of the story line, by continual deceptions to fool the reader into believing the heroes and villains are something other than they actually are. His one major fault as a writer is a certain sameness that pervades the entire body of his work. He has obviously recognized this deficiency, and has made a concerted attempt in his most recent books to vary the settings, plots, and characters stressed in his earlier novels.

I have attempted in this study to mention all of his novels that are available in the United States (one novel, *The Snow on the Ben*, has never been reprinted since its initial publication in 1961), and to analyze the techniques and devices that have made MacLean a success. This is, to the best of my knowledge, the first critical work to examine MacLean's fiction, but I'm certain it won't be the last: MacLean is too important an author to remain neglected for long.

Robert A. Lee
Redlands, California

THE WAR NOVELS

MacLean's first novel, *H.M.S. Ulysses*, though substantially different from his other books, does contain many elements typical of his later work. Certain aspects of structure reappear in all the books, and basic character types (such as the "rugged individualist") recur time and again in each of the novels. *Ulysses*' uniqueness lies in its semi-documentary nature. The scene is the North Atlantic during the second World War, where convoys are braving German raiders and submarines to bring supplies to the Russian Arctic port of Murmansk, Convoy FR 77, consisting of 35 freighters and the destroyer *Ulysses*, makes its tortuous way from Northern Scotland through the cold Arctic waters off Norway, losing all but five vessels in the process. The convoy provides MacLean with a convenient, linear plot structure: the action unfolds sequentially, with one brief flashback to give the reader background information on the *Ulysses*. The 16 chapters are identified by the time of day, ranging from the ships' Monday morning departure to the final arrival of the survivors in Murmansk on Sunday; the action of the novel exactly encompasses a week. A brief interlude near the center of the book, when the Captain of the destroyer inspects his ship, allows the reader time to "catch his breath" before being plunged once again into MacLean's maelstrom of action. Even in his first novel, MacLean has an acute sense of plot and structure, and it is clear that he understands quite well the consequences of action as defined by the necessities of storytelling.

This particular book is significant in other ways, too. The use of the sea as a character in itself is typical of MacLean's best work. The Atlantic storm is as terrifying and destructive as the German submarines and bombers. Man must not only combat other men, but also the impersonal forces of nature. MacLean is obviously following the old dictum, "write about what you know." He spent five years during World War

II as a torpedo man in the Royal Navy; he also acknowledges the assistance of his brother, a "master mariner," for technical help and advice. Throughout his long writing career, MacLean has been most successful when writing about the sea. There seems to be a certain structural advantage in having inanimate hazards sprinkled throughout the action, to allow the author to maintain the intense tone of his novel. And when he combines the threat of the sea with an Arctic milieu, the danger and jeopardy for his heroes seem even greater. The secret of MacLean's success as a suspense writer seems to lie in this juxtaposition of lone individual, enemy, and hostile natural forces. The resourceful man of action can triumph in the end, if his will and courage are strong enough; the rest will fall by the wayside. MacLean's heroes are strong men, who know themselves, and see the weaknesses in others; they survive because they want to.

This early apprentice piece differs from his later work in another respect. *Ulysses* has no central character or hero; the primary forces in the book are the ship, its crew, the enemy, and the sea/storm, all of which are impersonal to some degree. The point-of-view shifts back and forth among several figures, none of them more significant than the others. Captain Vallery, commander of the *Ulysses*, is noted for his wisdom and seamanship; his force of personality manages to mold the crew into an effective fighting force after the attempted mutiny with which the novel opens. Lt. Carpenter, the "Kapok Kid," is described as debonair, impeccably dressed, a marvel of seamanship, and an effective fighting man until his death in an air attack. Dr. Brooks, the ship's surgeon, figures prominently as the wise and humane medical officer who understands and counsels the crew. Seaman Ralston, one of the more memorable characters in the book, has lost most of his family to enemy attacks (his mother and sister were killed in air raids, and his brothers were sunk at sea); in a scene which verges on melodrama, he is later forced to torpedo one of the other ships in the convoy, which has been damaged by German raiders, and is now lighting up the remaining boats with its fire; the vessel is commanded by his father. Inevitably, Ralston himself must die in a later action, to complete the destruction of his family.

This brief rendition of the more prominent characters in the book delineates MacLean's difficulty in creating believable persons in his fiction. Too many of his characters are stereotypes: ship captains are strong and wise, able to unite their disgruntled sailors at a moment's notice; doctors are gentle, sage, and kind; brutal working-class sailors suddenly become noble patriots in the hour of need. And, since MacLean himself has popularized this particular kind of novel, it is easy to feel, as one reads through many of his books, that we've seen these people before, have experienced these scenes before, in a removed sort of *deja vu*. MacLean seems to have realized the samenesses in his books himself, for he has consciously tried to expand and diversify his fiction as his writing career has developed; unfortunately, his attempts to get away from the three basic settings of his novels, the sea, the war, and the Arctic, have generally proved to be failures, and in the end he always returns to the things he knows best.

Ulysses is also flawed in another sense. While the linear structure of the book is necessary to the plot, it also lends itself to cliched action; one by inevitable one, we meet nearly all the possible hazards, natural and man-made, of the typical sea story. Beginning with the officious bureaucracy of the Chief of Naval Operations, we rapidly encounter the mutiny, the first storm at sea (followed later, of course, by the greater storm), the sequential attacks by submarines, airplanes, more airplanes, more submarines, culminated by the potential threat of the German battleship *Tirpitz*, whose possible presence inspires the final despair among the men of the *Ulysses*. Although it never really appears (historically, it cannot), the battleship nonetheless represents a very damaging possibility.

What saves the novel from complete disaster is MacLean's ability to create memorable scenes, filled with extraordinary violence and bitterness. For example, one of the ships, the *Blue Ranger*, has been sunk, and its crew thrown into the chill

Arctic waters. Earlier in the book, MacLean noted that the sea brought an inevitable but curiously merciful death to any seamen forced to abandon ship; the extremely low temperatures of the water caused immediate shock and a quick death. To these wartime sailors, that promise of a swift end to their miseries provided some measure of consolation for the hazards of convoy duty. But the sailors of the *Blue Ranger* are thrown into a sea of fire, where the burning oil of their ship literally roasts them alive. "For a second a great gout of flame leapt up in the centre of the group, like a giant, incandescent magnesium flare, a flame that burnt the picture into the hearts and minds of the men on the bridge with a permanence and searing clarity that no photographic plate could ever have reproduced: men on fire, human torches beating insanely at the flames that licked, scorched and then incinerated clothes, hair and skin: men flinging themselves almost out of the water, backs arched like tautened bows, grotesque in convulsive crucifixion: men lying dead in the water, insignificant, featureless little oil-stained mounds in an oil-soaked plain: and a handful of fear-maddened men, faces inhumanly contorted, who saw the *Ulysses* and knew what was coming, as they frantically thrashed their way to a safety that offered only a few more brief seconds of unspeakable agony before they gladly died."

This is an extraordinary rendition, filled with violence and unforgetable metaphor. But MacLean makes it a wholly unique scene, by having Captain Vallery immediately turn his own ship, and send it straight through the horrible cluster of dying sailors, drowning them and cutting them up, and relieving them of the terrible misery of being burned alive. The men of the *Ulysses* "wept as pitiful, charred faces, turned up towards the *Ulysses* and alight with joy and hope, petrified into incredulous staring horror, as realisation dawned and the water closed over them; as hate-filled men screamed insane invective, both arms raised aloft, shaking fists white-knuckled through the dripping oil as the *Ulysses* tramped them under: as a couple of young boys were sucked into the maelstrom of the propellors, still giving the thumbs-up sign: as a particularly shocking case, who looked as if he had been barbecued on a spit and had no right to be alive, lifted a scorified hand to the blackened hole that had been his mouth, flung to the bridge a kiss in token of endless gratitude; and wept, oddly, most of all, at the inevitable humorist who lifted his fur cap high above his head and bowed gravely and deeply, his face into the water as he died." Such vividness is typical of MacLean at his best. At certain points in his books, scenes seem to leap out at the reader, lifting his fiction far above the ordinary tale of spies, war, and adventure. At times, in fact, one might almost think that MacLean had envisioned such passages first, before anything else, and later had created a plot just to give these remarkable renditions life and justification.

H.M.S. Ulysses contains some serious flaws, lapsing at times into melodrama and cliche, but it still has great power and effectiveness, even today. With its identification of certain character types, and its emphasis on a linear structure, it quite clearly points the way towards the writer MacLean will become in his later adventure novels. *Ulysses* was only moderately successful; MacLean's next book, however, proved to be his professional breakthrough as a writer.

The Guns of Navarone (1957) is MacLean's most famous and popular novel, and it was the first of his books to be made into a movie. In many ways, it stands as the prototype for all of his most successful work. Like *Ulysses*, the book is set during the second World War; however, MacLean has abandoned the documentary trappings of the earlier book (footnotes, for example), and has increased the emphasis on individual character, so obviously lacking in his first novel.

The Germans have constructed a "grim, impregnable iron fortress off the coast of Turkey," on an Aegean island that overlooks a crucial passageway. Keith Mallory, a famous New Zealand mountaineer, is sent with a mixed group of specially-trained and superbly qualified soldiers to put the fortress out of commission, so that 1200 Allied soldiers can be removed from a besieged island which can only be reached through the strait. The other members of the force include

Andy Stevens, navigator, "first-class alpinist," "fluent in both ancient and modern Greek," the typically young, enthusiastic, eager, and inevitably doomed figure so prominent in B movies; Dusty Miller, who is anti-military, but also "the finest saboteur in Southern Europe"; Casey Brown, a "born and ready-made engine room artificer" who is also a first-class guerrilla fighter; and finally, the super-partisan, Andrea, full of revenge for the crimes committed against his family. Once again, MacLean wanders on the verge of cliche. The characterizations are more fully developed in this book than in *Ulysses*, but they still tend to be stereotyped. One is reminded of some 1950s war flick which included the stock Jew, Pole, Italian, boy from Arkansas, and any number of other predictable and identifiable figures.

Because of its quick-moving, linear plot structure, and partially because it failed to focus on any one character, *Ulysses* contained little development of human emotion or motivation. The characters merely reacted to the stimuli around them. In *Navarone*, for the first time, MacLean begins building complex pictures of human feelings, even though these are necessarily relegated to the demands of plot and action. Early in the book he develops a theme which will dominate much of his fiction. The scaling of the cliff of Navarone is the high point of the novel, and, in fact, one of the great scenes out of the entire corpus of his work. As usual, MacLean paints an extraordinary visual picture of the perils and danger accompanying the climb up Navarone's sheer rock walls. He does this not by focusing on Mallory or Andrea, both of whom are expert climbers, but by concentrating on Andy Stevens, who, though "a first-class" mountaineer, is young and inexperienced. The motive he stresses is fear. "Fear. Terror. Panic. Do the thing you fear and the death of fear is certain. Do the thing you fear and the death of fear is certain. Once, twice, a hundred times, Andy Stevens repeated the words to himself, over and over again, like a litany. A psychiatrist had told him that once and he'd read it a dozen times since. Do the thing you fear and the death of fear is certain. The mind is a limited thing, they had said. It can only hold one thought at a time, one impulse to action. Say to yourself, I am brave, I am overcoming this fear, this stupid, unreasoning panic which has no origin except in my own mind, and because the mind can only hold one thought at a time, and because thinking and feeling are one, then you will be brave, you will overcome, and the fear will vanish like a shadow in the night. And so Andy Stevens said these things to himself, and the shadows only lengthened and deepened, lengthened and deepened, and the icy claws of fear dug ever more savagely into his dull exhausted mind, into his twisted, knotted stomach." The analysis of Stevens' fear is somewhat oversimplified. The cause, says MacLean, is Stevens' loss of self-respect, due to two acts of hesitation while fighting the enemy in actions prior to this climb. The inner battle of the man lies in the struggle between this loss of pride and the necessity to complete a mission on which 1200 lives depend. Thus Stevens climbs blindly upward. The issue can go one of two ways: either he may not be able to conquer his fears, and so will die two deaths, physical and spiritual; or, he may be able to control it, under the pressure of service to his fellow man, and so survive. MacLean lifts the struggle out of common stereotype by adding sheer physical fatigue, something which he will stress repeatedly in his later novels, particularly when natural forces are involved. Stevens is overwhelmed by exhaustion as he works his way towards the top, and this exhaustion gradually eats away his spirit, giving him an awareness of "nothing but the emptiness of it all, the emptiness and despair and the futility, the overwhelming lassitude and despair and his body slowly sinking down the face of the cliff." The fatigue leads to despair, the despair to self-defeat, and although there seems to be some loss of fear, he gives way to a "vast and heedless indifference," falls, and fractures his leg on the rocks below. From this point on Stevens is, of course, a burden to the rest of the group, and they must jeopardize themselves to protect him. He realizes this, sees himself as doomed, and finally redeems himself in self-sacrifice when he realizes his burden has become intolerable. Stevens goes gladly to his fate, reasserting his self-respect, and finally purging his soul of his fear: "Back where they had left him, Andy Stevens was lying on his stomach, peering down into the now almost dark ravine. There was no pain left in his body, none at all. He drew deeply on a cupped cigarette, smiled as he pushed another clip home into the magazine of the Bren. For the first time in his life Andy Stevens was happy and content beyond his understanding, a man at last at peace with himself. He was no longer afraid."

Other notable aspects in *Navarone* will recur throughout MacLean's other novels. Although an enemy is present, in this case the Germans, the enemy is never inherently evil. We have good Germans and bad Germans. On the one hand, the sadist, Skoda, murders and tortures with the best of them; but there is also the good soldier, Lt. Turzig, who fights with the Nazis, but will have nothing to do with the criminal or inhumane element. Similarly, the English side has its share of incompetents and undesirables. Early in the book, Captain Briggs, a formal and bureaucratic man, refuses to believe that a man caught listening at the door as Mallory's group makes its plans could be a German agent; Briggs frees the man, and the agent subsequently jeopardizes the entire mission. MacLean never hesitates to lambast the bureaucratic fools who inhabit the official structures of government and the military. His heroes are always unconventional individualists who work outside and around governmental regulations. The contrast between the free-thinking hero and the stuffy, pompous soldier is striking.

Another recurring theme of MacLean's work appears for the first time in this book. As the group makes its tortuous way across the island, they are accompanied by Greek partisans, one of whom is working against them. In this novel, the traitor is fairly obvious to the careful reader, but in later books MacLean will become adept at disguising the villain more carefully. In fact, as the novels grow more complex, the traitor-in-the-midst becomes the central mystery of many of the books: the adventure gives way to the puzzle story. In *Navarone*, however, Panayis is so sadistic and filled with hate, and so described in terms of evilness and viciousness that it comes as no surprise when he is found to be the double agent in Mallory's group. He meets, of course, a suitable fate.

The crucial scene in the book, the ruining of the fortress, is particularly well-handled, although it probably is more vivid in the movie version, where the special effects, explosions, and exchanges of gunfire make a stunning visual display. In the book, the denouement does not seem to have quite the impact that the cliff-scaling had, perhaps because the focus in the earlier sections was on specific individuals, and their reactions to a tense and dangerous situation, while in the later parts, the action is on a grander scale, and seems to move ahead almost on its own accord. This is a key to MacLean's work. As he develops his writing skills, he becomes most effective in those scenes where the individual hero is either struggling with himself, struggling with others, or struggling with nature. The key battle is man against himself.

Although it is not his best book, *The Guns of Navarone*, MacLean's first real novel, is important in setting the stage for the later (and better) books. All the elements are present in this novel: the inner struggle of the heroes, the deception at the center of the plot structure, the gradual development of characters capable of feeling complex human emotions and motivations. The later books will simply elaborate on them. At the same time, it is also evident that MacLean is still learning his craft. For all of the book's driving action and grand suspense, it contains a certain artificiality that is almost inhuman. The dialogue often sounds like speeches staged between automatons, and we seldom feel that we are really seeing characters thinking their innermost thoughts. Everything is exaggerated: the guns are the biggest guns around; Mallory is the greatest mountaineer available; Andrea is the bravest and most indomitable of men, minor characters and situations suffer from excesses. For example, when Mallory is thinking about Louki, the loyal Greek who accompanies the men on their mission, he says: "Still gazing out the windowless hole in the wall at the fortress gate, Mallory found himself hoping intensely that nothing would happen to the sad-eyed little Greek, and not only because in his infinite resource and local knowledge he had been invaluable to them and was likely to prove so again; all these considerations apart, Mallory had formed the deepest affection for him, for his unvarying cheerfulness, his enthusiasm, his eagerness to help and to please, above all for his complete disregard of self." The world of *Navarone* is a world of extremes. Such excesses are common to the suspense novel, where the writer often feels that simple terror and action will not suffice. Unfortunately, the usual result is characterizations that are bigger-than-life, cardboard figures, overblown situations, with an emphasis on plot rather than people. At this point in his career, MacLean is still grappling with these kinds of problems.

A brief word should be said at this point about *Force 10 from Navarone*, a sequel published some eleven years later, in 1968. An attempt to cash in on the success of the earlier book, it can only be viewed as an artistic failure, MacLean's poorest novel thus far. The action picks up immediately from the conclusion of the first book. Mallory, Miller, and Andrea are rescued at sea, and given a new mission, involving Yugoslav partisans and the German forces in the Balkans. Typical MacLean deceits are used to get the Germans to remove their troops from the area. The climax features the mining and destruction of a dam, and the flooding of a German division. Intermingled with the actions scenes are all familiar trademarks: mistaken identities, false roles, jeopardies, hazards, and danger, all of which our intrepid heroes overcome. And at the end of the book, the three are once again congratulated for a successful mission: they have made the "deception complete." But the conceits have become almost silly in this book. A blind Yugoslavian minstrel, who goes around the partisan camps strumming "old Bosnian love songs," turns out to be the "Head of British espionage in the Balkans;" his sister, who guides him around the camps like some friendly dog, turns out to be his wife.

The novel is saved from total disaster by one striking

scene, which may be as visually impressive and imaginative as anything MacLean has ever written. At one point, in order to fashion a landing strip out of the winter countryside, hundreds of Yugoslav soldiers troop back and forth across the snow-laden hills, stomping down the snow so that a plane can land without floundering. One character equates it to a scene from Dante's *Inferno*, only "a hundred degress colder." Unfortunately, this section is not enough to save the book from itself, and by the large, the work is overly familiar, and rather choppy, as MacLean skips back and forth from one group of characters to another. Sequels are rarely as successful as the original, and this book only proves the rule.

MacLean's third novel, *South by Java Head* (1958), also features World War II as the primary setting. MacLean returns to the sea, the locale of his first book, and it's quite clear that he's done his homework, tracing the route of the novel from Singapore south towards the island of Sumatra and then into the Indian Ocean. MacLean has always been extremely careful in checking details which less conscious writers might overlook; one has the feeling in reading this book that the author has either been there himself, or knows the area well enough to extrapolate from researched data.

The story uses one of the adventure writer's stock situations, the escape motif. In 1942, Singapore is being overrun by the Japanese; a group of people escape from the city, and flee towards Australia. The assorted group of characters include a child; a Danish nurse, who bears a hideous scar on her face from a Japanese bayonet; von Effen, the Dutchman; and Brigadier Farnholme, a pukka sahib, who seems to have been included to parody the English colonial mentality. They escape the advancing enemy forces in a derelict ex-slave trader, the *Kerry Dancer*, then hit the ever-present typhoon, founder on a reef, and are finally rescued by an oil tanker. The first office of the tanker is John Nicolson, the central figure of the novel. The survivors of the trader have no sooner been rescued than the new vessel is attacked by Japanese zeros, and immediately goes to the bottom. The refugees take to the sea in life boats. And now the action begins.

In a scene which strains the credulity of the reader to the utmost, the men on the life boat managed to cripple a Japanese submarine, killing many of its crew. Fleeing to a nearby island, they are again attacked by the enemy, but make a miraculous escape, and once again turn to the sea. MacLean concentrates on one particular boat, which includes Farnholme, whom we now learn is the chief English espionage agent in Southeast Asia; Captain Siran, the evil skipper of the *Kerry Dancer*, together with some of his crew; and McKinnon, a typical MacLean type who is described as "old, unchangeable, apparently indestructible," with "a soft voice and the gun always in his hand." McKinnon is the strong and loyal serviceman, a type who appears in many of the author's books. The common man is the only person who stands fast in a changing world. MacLean would apparently wish us to think of the average man as the moral alternative to the deceit of bureaucracy and sophistication.

Farmholme is carrying the secret Japanese plans for the invasion of Australia, and must deliver them to the allied forces in that country before they're implemented. Unfortunately, the group of wanderers is finally captured by the enemy. The deceptions begin to multiply. Farnholme pretends to be a Japanese collaborator, and goes to a sacrificial death, destroying a torpedo boat in the process. The group befriends some Sumatran natives, only to be turned in by them to the enemy soldiers; subsequently, however, we learn that Captain Siran was responsible for the treason. Von Effen, we find, is not a Dutchman, but a high-ranking German intelligence officer, who has been pursuing both the invasion plans and some diamonds which Farnholme carried in his possession. In a neat series of twists, the mystery of the story unfolds, about 30 pages before the end of the book. By this time, we know who is who, and which side they are working for. The group escapes from the Japanese. Interestingly, they are aided in this attempt by von Effen, who knows that the Japanese captain (whose son was too coincidentally killed on the submarine) will murder and torture the hostages in revenge. Von Effen rebels, giving up his life in the process, so the good guys can exit with their skins intact. Von Effen is clearly a German with a conscience, who believes in his pride, but who is not willing to commit murder to win the war. As he says: " 'We Germans do not go easily. This is not the end of von Effen.' He paused for a long moment, went on in a whisper. 'Winning a war costs a great deal. It always costs a great deal. But sometimes the cost is too high, and it is not worth the price. Tonight the cost, the price asked, was far too high. I — I could not pay the price.' "

South by Java Head represents a further development of MacLean's skills. The characters are more interesting than those in his two earlier books. John Nicolson, for example, has a human dimension rarely seen in *Navarone*. Similarly, the ancillary characters are just off-beat enough to move them out of the stereotypes that many adventure novelists, MacLean included, are always in danger of creating. The action is fast-paced, the descriptions of action well-handled. The most interesting facet of the book is the thread of deceit that runs throughout the novel. MacLean had used character deception before (in *Navarone*, for example, Andrea played a sniveling and cowardly Greek when captured by the Germans), but this is the first time that he has consciously employed the technique to further the suspense of the book. At least four of the major characters in *Java* are eventually shown to be something other than what they pretended to be at the beginning of the book. This, coupled with the many twists and turns MacLean throws at his readers as the group runs from the Japanese, is captured and freed, recaptured and refreed, becomes MacLean's standard technique in most of his later books. He continually attempts to deceive the reader in an elaborate masquerade which is, when successful, a masterful way of maintaining the suspense of the story, and when unsuccessful, becomes mere trickery for its own sake. His best books are those which keep the reader guessing until the very end of the story.

MacLean's philosophy in these three early novels is conservative, nationalistic, and oriented towards an acceptance of authority. To some extent, this probably is due to the subject matter of the books; each takes place during the second World War, and military necessity demands the following of orders without question. In all three books, it is clear that the allies are the "good guys," and the Germans the "bad." MacLean does make some effort, though, to delineate certain levels of performance in each group: not all Germans are evil per se, and not all Britons are heroes. *H.M.S. Ulysses* opens with the senior officers in the British Naval Command unable to understand the reasons for the short-lived mutiny on the ship (the sailors are exhausted from constant duty without any opportunity for rest and recuperation); the book closes with the same officers failing to perceive the enormous gallantry of the vessel, and planning to cover up the story of its heroism. Mallory in *Navarone* shows some small signs of rebellion, and Andrea represents an individual unfettered by bureaucratic niceties. The tone of *Navarone* is anti-establishment only within the essentially favorable portrait of a military organization. Still, the emphasis in this book is clearly on individual effort: the job can only be done by specially-trained agents; the average soldier just isn't enough. In MacLean's third book, the leading character, Nicolson, is a private seaman, with no naval connections whatever; even more interestingly, von Effen, the German spy, is essentially heroic, self-sacrificing, and by far the most intriguing person in the book, and the most complex. The "evil" people are sprinkled evenly on both sides, including the two captains.

MacLean's emphasis has shifted significantly through the course of these three novels, from collective action to individual will. And while the essentially conservative values of society are not really questioned here — the allies are always right — the maintenance of these values is left in the hands of the individual working on the fringes of a society that really doesn't approve such actions. In short, MacLean is working towards and within a common literary tradition, the definition of literary heroism as the conflict between an uneasy accomodation of private action and the public good.

THE SECRET AGENTS

In *South by Java Head*, MacLean focuses on an individual in a way he didn't in his first two books, where the war and action were in themselves major forces, acting against any central figure. John Nicholson of *Java* is brought into the story almost casually, and although he becomes the major character in the book, receiving praise even from the enemy, the other persons detract somewhat from his image, because of their unique personalities. Farnholme, the Danish nurse, Farnholme's wife, or even von Effen, the German intelligence agent, all seem more interesting as people. Nevertheless, MacLean seemed to have realized in this book that a central figure was necessary to give his books a coherence around which he could build a believable plot, and through which he could lead us into layers of revelation and suspense. Therefore, in his next five novels, two of which rank among his best, MacLean focuses very directly on either an indomitable secret agent (the hero of the novel), a first person narrator, or sometimes a combination of both. Character has superseded action per se. In addition, the war has been temporarily abandoned; evidently, MacLean felt he was getting into a rut, because he doesn't come back to the war milieu for quite some time. In the sequence of five novels beginning with *The Secret Ways*, the scene shifts from Eastern Europe, and the smuggling of a scientist out of Hungary, to the Arctic, to a Pacific island, and finally, in *The Golden Rendezvous*, to a luxury liner on the Carribean. These novels represent MacLean at the height of his powers. His apprentice period has passed, and he is clearly stretching his abilities to their furthest extent. Two of the novels, *Night Without End* and *The Golden Rendezvous*, are as good as anything he has written.

The Secret Ways, a more accurate and interesting title than the British version, *The Last Frontier* (1959), is a mediocre novel, but notable for its introduction of the secret agent into MacLean's fiction. Michael Reynolds, "Britain's top agent," has been assigned the task of rescuing a British scientist who had defected to Hungary. Other than one piece of daring-do on the top of a speeding railroad train, a scene which anticipates a more successful version in *Breakheart Pass*, and an uninspiring bit of torture when Reynolds is captured, the action is rather tame for MacLean, and the novel is comparatively insipid. To some degree, this is a result of the locale, urban Budapest and assorted Hungarian villages and landscapes. The reliance on natural violence that we have seen so many times in the past is completely lacking, and it shows. The perils are relatively small, the fear under control, the terror rather minor. All the action flows from the conflict between the agent (and his allies, the freedom-fighting Hungarians) and their communist antagonists. And these human battles seem curiously bloodless by comparison.

MacLean is also more loquacious than usual; several speeches go on for pages at a time, completely discarding the pretence of a normal conversation. They seem to have been inserted into the book merely to inform the reader of MacLean's version of history. We are apprised of the many brutalities perpetuated by the Germans and Russians in the War, and then given a list of each country's sins. Towards the end of the novel, one of the characters makes a long political speech in which he castigates various nations for their political and social errors, from the Ku Klux Klan and racial prejudice in America, to British colonialism, to Eastern European brutality. The only solution offered in return is "compassion," a rather banal response.

Another fault of the book is the cliched nature of the characters. Jansci, the martyr figure in the novel, has been tortured for his political beliefs, and suffered all the indignities that can be put upon a man. He is described thusly by Reynolds: "A lined, tired face, a middle-aged face that belied the thick, snow-white hair above, a face deeply, splendidly etched by experience, by a sorrowing and suffering such as Reynolds could not even begin to imagine, it held more goodness, more wisdom and tolerance and understanding than

Reynolds had ever seen in the face of any man before. It was the face of a man who had seen everything, known everything, and experienced everything and still had the heart of a child." His friend, "the Count," who is equally as talented a fighter, is renowned for his disguises, and is called by MacLean "a born aristocrat," which is, after all, what we assume a count must be. Jansci also has a noble and long-suffering wife (naturally), and a beautiful daughter, who at the end of the book marches off hand in hand with the secret agent to the safety of the West. Undoubtedly, they live happily ever after.

The book is interesting in one respect, however, since we have more of MacLean's political philosophy before us than ever before. Early in the book, Reynolds reveals to Jansci that they are going to trick the British professor Jennings into returning to England by claiming his wife is ill. Jansci says this is a despicable trick, and cannot be justified by any ethical standard. Reynolds professes the amoral indifference of the secret agent. Later, however, perhaps as a result of all the preaching about equal brutality between nations, Reynolds does come to an awareness of ends and means, and in a surprising scene, spares the life of the cruel Hungarian communist, Colonel Hidas. It may be unwise to make too much of this; MacLean's political romanticism extolls the virtues of justice and mercy, and despises the vices of brutality and tyranny, attitudes which are conventional and unsurprising, and undoubtedly aimed at a certain kind of audience. Although there are good and bad communists, and good and bad British spies, MacLean is obviously not going to rock the boat too much, since he is first and foremost a professional, and the professional's primary aim is selling books. Nationalism is overtly despised, and the political opinions expressed are neither persuasive nor totally consistent. Unfortunately, the long speeches tend to get in the way of what little action there is in this book, and retard the plot even more than usual. By any standard, *The Secret Ways* is one of MacLean's weaker efforts, and although it contains certain values that are interesting in their relationship to his other writings, they do not save the book from being over-written, over-long, and probably over-praised.

In sharp contrast, *Night Without End* (1960) is the first of MacLean's novels to use first person narration. And, excepting *Ulysses*, it is also the first of his books to be set in the Arctic, to which he has returned time and again in more recent works. For the first time, MacLean uses a physician as the central figure in the book, a technique he will employ most successfully in *Bear Island*. But *Night* ranks as one of MacLean's best books for other reasons: the combination of an exciting, imaginative plot, interesting characters, the antagonism of the Arctic climate, and the skillful masquerading of the real purposes of people left to their own devices.

The plot is simple and straightforward. A chartered airliner crashes under odd circumstances on the Greenland icecap, some 400 miles above the Arctic circle, near a station of International Geophysical Year scientists. Dr. Mason, the narrator of the novel, rescues the survivors of the accident, together with his aide, Jackstraw, a native Greenlander. Following the crash, strange things begin to happen. The radio transmitter is smashed, there's a fire in the station, peculiar accidents begin affecting the rescue vehicles. Finally, one of the survivors is murdered. All of these incidents are effectively communicated through the mind of Mason, whose perceptive eyes report everything he sees, tinted with a proper sense of perplexity.

Equally important are the descriptions of the harsh Arctic climate. MacLean manages this in exceptional fashion. The hostile natural terrain is presented with a mixture of factual data and rhetorical dynamics that is credible, impressive, and inspiring. We learn, for example, that *sastrugi* are regular undulations in the frozen snow, a phenomenon which causes the party great difficulties in later journeys; the brief but intense Arctic storms are williwaws. The repeated emphasis on the dangers of low temperature environments, combined with extended narratives of what the winds and ice can do, make the scene believable and awe-inducing.

The essence of MacLean's best work is found in the mixture of natural and human terrors. He throws together an extremely hostile climate with an equally malevolent group of people, and the result is fear, terror, a sense of impending death, and high suspense, all of which is communicated to the reader through his jumble of characters. This book is a particularly fine example of how MacLean meshes the two disparate elements to produce a unified whole. The characters are never allowed to sit still, except for dramatic effect, and by inference, neither is the reader. In *Ulysses*, the Germans and the sea were equally hostile to the allied cause, but each seemed to work separately, to be confronted on its own distinct terms. In *Java*, the Japanese were an ever-present threat, but the weather, although it caused the refugees some problems early in the story, really wasn't much of a factor. *Navarone* includes both natural forces and human, but each is dealt with separately; Mallory's crew first fights its way up the cliffs, and then goes after the Germans. The coherent combination of hostile environment and hostile enemies arrayed against a common human foe is successfully wrought for the first time in *Night Without End*. Each event follows on the other, and builds the suspense. After the crew member's murder, the party must leave the station, because of threatening weather, and a limited food supply. During the flight across the ice cap towards the home station, the "accidents" continue to happen, and it becomes clear that someone among them is trying to sabotage the tractors, and eliminate the entire group, for reasons unknown. Mason's party must fight off threats external and internal to survive, without knowing why they are being subjected to an unreasonable kind of punishment. The shadow of death is never far away. Roughly two-thirds of the way through the book, we finally discover the key: the plane was carrying the plans for a "super-secret guided missile mechanism." Interestingly, MacLean spends little time explaining the specifics of the device, and it really isn't necessary to the story line. The device is only the trigger, the rationale that causes a series of automatic reactions amongst the characters. The natural and human antagonisms that result matter more than the cause does.

The first person narration works perfectly in this kind of story. Mason is knowledgeable about the Arctic and its dangers, but is not immune to them. He suffers from the cold as much as "the Queen of the Musical Comedy Stage," one of the survivors of the wrecked plane. On the other hand, he knows enough to speak authoritatively of the dangers of the storms and cold, and so render those perils believable to us. Mason also serves as a foil for the mysterious events which follow the plane crash: he is understandably worried and perplexed, but his training as a doctor, and his understanding of the circumstances, permit a skeptical and insightful response to the situation. MacLean lets Mason, and therefore us, discover what is happening as it happens, but Mason's superior position allows a certain amount of introspection and judgment to enter in. At the same time, we are really listening to the thoughts of a fallible man, and so the author can legitimately withhold certain details and judgments that Mason can't see or make. And sometimes, Mason himself fails to voice thoughts or suspicions he may have; this technique is perfected justified, for it maintains the doctor's central position in the novel, enhances his intelligence, and at the same time keeps just enough evidence away from the reader to maintain the drama of the story. Eventually, of course, the communist agents reveal themselves, and, in an ironic comment against the socialist dogma, turn out to be the two passengers purporting to be a minister and the manager of a tractor factory. Deception is a central fixture of this kind of novel. There is a final, somewhat melodramatic, fight on the side of the glacier between Mason and Smallwood, the agent/minister; the scene is a fitting climax to a novel full of such adventurous incidents.

One final comment. Unlike *The Secret Ways*, *Night Without End* contains little of the political speeches which marred the former. This is a story of survival in a struggle against the forces of destruction; political theorizing and social commentary have little part in such a book, and MacLean wisely decides not to let either Mason or Smallwood make any judgments about the plans for the missile system, or about the societies which spawned such creations. The key elements in any good adventure are struggle and conflict, and MacLean uses both to create a minor masterpiece of suspense writing.

The Black Shrike (1961), which was originally published in England as *The Dark Crusader*, was the first MacLean novel to be issued under a pseudonym. MacLean used the name Ian Stuart on three books, including this book, *The Snow on the Ben* (a book virtually unknown in this country, and the only one of MacLean's fictions never to be reprinted), and *The Satan Bug*. All except the middle novel have been reprinted since under MacLean's real name. The pseudonym was apparently used because 1961 and 1962 were the first (and only) years in which he produced more than one novel. It was perhaps felt by his publishers that the market could not support two MacLean novels a year, and that a penname would help.

Shrike continues the technique of the first person narrator. But in this book, instead of the outsider accidentally involved in matters beyond his control, we have the superior British agent, Bentall. His mission concerns the mysterious disappearances of certain English nuclear scientists, who are apparently responding to advertisements for a special scientific program in Australia; the inference is, of course, that they are being abducted by some unknown foreign power to be used for its nefarious schemes. The Black Shrike is a missile, and the scene is set on a South Pacific island, similar to that in *Java Head*. Unfortunately, the book seems flat after the excitement of *Night*, with little real peril, and a minor plot. The one interesting aspect of this minor MacLean saga concerns Bentall's meeting with the head of the Secret Service, Colonel Raine, before being sent on his mission. Towards the end of the novel, we discover that Raine is a double agent, and that the entire affair was created by him to protect his cover. Hence, the story is in itself a double hoax, both to the reader and to Bentall, who has undergone his trial on a fraudulent premise. On the other hand, the idea of the head of the service being a counter-agent is bizarre enough to provide a most engaging and attractive twist to the plot that is unique in MacLean's fiction, and infrequent in the entire spy genre. The one part of the book that is the most intriguing is ironically the one part that destroys the integrity of the novel, and the action which it encompasses, leaving us with a somewhat forced plot, not up to the level of the books which precede or follow it.

Fear Is the Key, also published in 1961, is the third novel in a row to employ the first person technique. The book opens with Talbot, the narrator, waiting for a plane bearing his family and a smuggled cargo to land; but the craft is attacked and shot down and everyone aboard is killed. Several years later, Talbot has become an entirely different person from the sympathetic father/husband figure of the prologue. Now a cop killer, Talbot escapes from the rural southern courtroom where he is being tried, kidnapping an innocent bystander, in direct contradiction to our initial impressions of his character. Alert readers of MacLean will recognize one of the author's deceptions: obviously, one way or the other, Talbot is not the person he's pictured to be. Talbot shoots a policeman in the course of his escape, further establishing his credentials as a law-breaker. A spectacular car chase ensues, in which Talbot steals several automobiles, and runs a number of road blocks. He hides his kidnap victim in a nearby motel, but is suddenly confronted by Jablonsky, an apparent blackmailer. Jablonsky overcomes Talbot, no small feat, and begins extorting money from the father of the kidnapped girl, General Blair Ruthven, "excepting maybe Paul Getty . . . the richest oil man in the United States." Now the twists and turns in the plot begin piling one on top of another. The two men and the girl go to Ruthven's estate, where the General is surrounded by an number of criminal types. Within the space of a few pages, we suddenly discover that Jablonsky is a cop, and then a crooked cop, which seems to satisfy Ruthven and his friends. Jablonsky is made Talbot's guard. But it quickly becomes clear that Jablonsky and Talbot, instead of being antagonists, are really allies of a sort, or even colleagues. The motivation is always kept unclear, and each of the characters is surrounded in mystery. Ruthven should be a rich, patriarchal figure, maybe even a parody of the Southern aristocrat with the ritual military title. Instead, he seems intimidated by those supposedly working for him on his estate. Talbot's alliances are unknown, except his obvious association with Jablonsky. But Jablonsky is either a policeman, a corrupt policeman, or something inbetween.

Jablonsky is murdered, and Mary Ruthven and Talbot join forces, as the forces of good and evil begin to sort themselves out. Assisting the "good guys" is Kennedy, Mary's chauffeur, who seems to be something more than that, and who clearly loves her. The role of the General remains shadowy, even to his daughter. He may be a willing companion of the villains, Vyland and Royale, or he may have a knife at his back, literally or figuratively. The purposes of the criminals remains obscure; at this point, halfway through the book, we still have no idea what crimes are being committed, what's at stake, and what relationship all of this has to the curious prologue. The knowledge is gradually uncovered like the leaves of an onion, piece by piece. Talbot is clearly an agent, but of what or for whom is uncertain; he obviously has some kind of personal stake in the business. MacLean has combined the techniques of using either the individual accidently involved in things which he doesn't understand, or the agent sent directly out to do job; Talbot is both. His "agentness" gradually becomes clear as the plot unfolds, but it's never rammed down the reader's throat. We see him act, and come to respect his actions, knowledge, and deeds; but we are never told by some outside source how superior he is to everyone else. His human side remains believable throughout the book. Action has supplanted rhetoric, giving us one of MacLean's best characterizations.

The mystery is finally resolved in the last third of the book, when the focus of novel switches to one of Ruthven's oil-drilling platforms in the Gulf of Mexico. The platform is merely a subterfuge to hide an underwater expedition sent to salvage the treasure from a wrecked airplane, obviously the craft mentioned in the prologue. Suddenly the motivations of Talbot become clear: he is indeed an agent, but he is also pursuing, in revenge, those who shot down his brother, wife, and son. This revelation comes in an exciting scene, when Talbot descends to the seabed with Vyland and Royale in a bathysphere; Talbot says he's going to kill all three of them, and tricks the two confederates into confessing their sins, at the same time activating the radio link with the surface. Central to the scene is the element of fear. The imminent suffocation and drowning affects Vyland and Royale in such a way that their desperation prompts an accounting that they never would have given under normal circumstances. The terror of the deeps is more excruciating than the fear of man. Counterpointed around this scene are others, including one where Talbot fights one of the criminals to the death on a platform high over the derrick. In a sense, MacLean is resorting to all the conventional action scenes to liven up the novel; but the personal involvement of Talbot communicates itself to the reader, and makes what might otherwise be a run-of-the-mill adventure novel dynamic and stimulating. For example, Talbot's pretented willingness to kill himself along with the criminals in the bathysphere seems entirely credible when described in the context of Talbot's retelling of his child's death. This human element, well disguised throughout the book, gives the final scene a power and force which is clearly missing in *The Black Shrike* or *The Secret Ways.*

The ending is similarly well handled. With all the villains either dead or about to be executed, and with the relationship between Mary and Kennedy a constant possibility, Talbot, once again alone, without his family or even Jablonsky, simply walks "stiffly" back to his hotel. The understated denouement, the lack of any sense of triumph, gives this novel a poignancy that is rare in MacLean's fiction. *Fear Is the Key* ranks as one of his best efforts to date.

The Golden Rendezvous (1962) brings to a conclusion a

period of writing which includes some of MacLean's most successful and effective books. Like his preceding novels, this work uses first-person narration. The action of the novel takes place on a Caribbean luxury liner, the most exclusive and expensive boat of its kind, where the average meal is "something for even the most blase epicure to dream about." The S.S. *Campari* caters to an exclusive class of millionaires and jet-setters. But if the setting is exotic and unusual, the story is not. The narrator, the ship's first officer, is thrown into the action through happenstance. The specific mystery is kept well-hidden until midway through the book, although the suspense doesn't really approach that of *Fear* or *Night*. As he has done before, MacLean titles each chapter with sequential time frames, to stress the linear nature of the plot, and increase tension.

At the center of the book lies the theft and presence of a stolen guided missile. The remaining elements are familiar to readers of MacLean. The heroine is a daughter of one of the rich men on board ship; Carter, the first officer, is single, and not a widower, as in many previous books, and the love element is inevitable. The action begins with the destruction of the ship's radio, and the murder of a crew member. Captain Bullen is blustery and gruff, but also (typically) kindly and fundamentally wise. Again typically, the villains are perhaps more interestingly drawn personalities than the heroes. The "bad guys" in this case are associated with a political revolution in a Caribbean country. To support the revolution, they need to hijack a cargo of gold, and to get the gold, the guided missile is utterly necessary. MacLean also throws in his usual hurricane for good measure.

The Golden Rendezvous is competent but redundant. Taken on its own terms, it works as a taut, suspenseful adventure story, good for a couple of hours reading, but no more. The feeling of self-jeopardy on the part of the hero is present, but not strongly stressed. The book merely continues the techniques and inventions that MacLean has developed in earlier fictions.

TRANSITIONS

The Satan Bug (1962), which was issued first under the pseudonym Ian Stuart, can most profitably be viewed as a transitional novel in MacLean's carrer. Following the apprenticeship of his first three novels, MacLean wrote a series of generally successful adventures that made his name as a suspense writer. With this new book, MacLean now begins a period of writing which either recapitulates the World War II settings of his first few books, or follows the Cold War milieu so well established in his second cycle of novels. One almost gets the feeling here that MacLean was finding it difficult to come up with new ideas which would inspire his writing. Having written nine novels, and explored the limits of the conventional adventure, he either had to venture into areas he knew little about, or rehash plots and ideas that he had already used in previous books. As we shall see, this difficulty becomes more pronounced as his career advances.

The quality of these transitional novels is generally high, although they seem to lack the imaginative spark that permeated the earlier works. *Satan* continues the use of the first-person narrator, and once again deals with a secret agent. But the special operative in this case, Pierre Cavell, is not as bloodless or uninteresting as his two predecessors, Bentall and Reynolds. MacLean gives Cavell a personal stake in the matter, for while the essence of the conflict is politics, the agent's wife is caught up in the struggle, and his exploits to save her become as crucial to the reader as any social or political ideology.

As the title implies, the threat involves the possibility of an extremely dangerous biological germ being released in urban London. The city setting removes the element of natural threat that has played such a large role in MacLean's books, and necessarily lessens the possibilities of fear and terror. The conflict revolves around Cavell, Scarlatti (the villain), and the British Army Intelligence Service. The one memorable scene in the novel has Scarlatti and the agent fighting over botulinous toxin and the Satan Bug in a helicopter in flight. Scarlatti is subdued, London is saved, and the criminal steps out of the copter to his death, rather than face the likelihood of a jail term. The sympathy that this action engenders in the reader speaks much for MacLean's abilities as a writer. One can see his humanity amidst the villainy of his character.

Despite Cavell's personal involvement in the struggle, the emphasis in this book has shifted back towards social commentary. The book contains nothing of the didactics of *The Secret Ways*, but the counterplay is clearly East set against West in the struggle for political supremacy throughout the world. Three of MacLean's next four novels feature many of the same elements.

Several of MacLean's books have been made into movies, many of them with the author himself collaborating in the writing of the screen play, or in advising the directors during actual shooting. And since much of his writing is inherently cinematic, the translations from page to screen have, on the whole, been quite successful. The one exception to this rule is *Ice Station Zebra*. Most of the films have remained quite faithful to the original books, and this may, perhaps, have contributed to their success, because MacLean has an excellent sense of the drama of fear, and few movie makers have been able to do more than try to match his effectiveness. But *Zebra* was significantly altered in the transition, totally destroying the sense of the novel; the result bears only faint resemblance to the book version. In addition, the film was badly directed and acted, adding to the chaotic effect. The book deserved better.

The first-person point-of-view is maintained, and a physician serves as hero/narrator. The setting is the Arctic. When these tried and true techniques are combined with an exotic situation, a nuclear submarine in jeopardy, the result is bound to be fast-paced, exciting adventure. MacLean is able to maintain the credibility of an otherwise highly improbable situation by infusing just enough technology and arcane information about nuclear vessels to give the plot a versimilitude it otherwise would not have. The technique of false starts and deception operates from the beginning.

Dr. Carpenter arrives in the Arctic to accompany a nuclear submarine on a rescue mission to a floating station on the ice. It is apparent from the beginning that Carpenter is not quite what he seems; similarly, the station itself, the Zebra of the title, is a mask for something else. But Carpenter's real identity, that of a British secret agent, is not the center of the puzzle, nor is the secret of the station itself very surprising. Indeed, MacLean almost seems to stumble in this book. Carpenter tells the American commander of the sub several different tales, meanwhile admitting in asides to the reader that none of these is the real truth of the matter; in fact, the stories turn out to be so close to the mystery that the apparent misleading elements of the novel are really the clues to its final resolution. The rescue mission has nominally been arranged to recover secret information being obtained by the station on Russian military secrets. To the reader, however, the real mystery involves the traitor-within-the-midst that MacLean has so successfully employed before: who and what has caused the emergency aboard Ice Station Zebra?

Strangely, the specific facts seem to matter very little in this book. As the submarine makes its journey under the ice, and the details begin unfolding, the hazards of the mission are emphasized through a series of mishaps. The romantic lure of the Arctic, and the unique situation of a nuclear submarine crawling beneath the undersea mounds of ice hold the reader's attention longer than the plot might warrant in other circumstances. MacLean employs the natural forces of the cold climate to good advantage. The submarine surfaces close to the camp, and the race is on, through a blinding snow storm, to rescue the men of Ice Station Zebra. On the return voyage, a fire breaks out on the sub while it is still below the ice cap, and unable to surface; the threat of death is ever-present. While this is not MacLean's best fusion of natural hazards and man-made antagonism, certain scenes come close to his peak;

the fire, for example, was set by a traitor as vulnerable to death as his potential victims. And once set, the flames are very difficult to control. The character of Dr. Carpenter shows the same judicious use of the first-person narrator that MacLean has developed in the past: Carpenter reveals just enough of the plot to entice the reader on, and at the same time maintains a sympathetic personality through whom we can view the perils as they're thrown at us. The fact that the villain of the book turns out to be another doctor is a minor fillip that MacLean no doubt finds delightful. The American sailors are discreetly drawn, and as far from the standard novel cliches as MacLean can manage. The surprises are kept at arm's length until just before the end of the book, maintaining the suspense throughout. Even when the book becomes tired and over-long, the basic situations are so competently handled that they carry the day. Alistair MacLean has obviously developed a certain measure of confidence as a writer; the only question remaining, both to him and to us, is continuity of performance. Can he keep coming up with new and exciting ideas?

At this point in his career, Alistair MacLean has reached the top of his profession. Each of his books is eagerly awaited by a growing number of fans in the United States and Britain; henceforward, he is virtually writing for a guaranteed audience, a situation all professional writers aspire to attain. Interestingly, it is precisely at this high point in his career that there is a three-year gap in his publications. His next novel, *When Eight Bells Toll*, does not appear until 1966. All the familiar elements, the first-person narrator, the secret agent, the hiding of roles, the postponement of the denouement until the last few chapters, are present in this novel. And, though familiar by now, they are all nonetheless effective, and this novel is one of MacLean's most interesting adventure stories.

The premise of *Eight Bells* is the piracy of gold-carrying ships by a wealthy shipping magnate, Skouras. The agent, Calvert, attempts to recover the gold against a background of the rugged Scottish coast, terrain MacLean is obviously familiar with. The novel opens with Calvert investigating one of the suspect ships at night, and finding two of his comrades dead; he is assaulted by the crew, and just makes his escape. What makes the scene particularly effective is the familiar MacLean technique of reserving the rationale, and hiding the facts in such a way that the reader does not know whom or what Calvert is pursuing, or exactly what the situation is. *Eight Bells* has more than its normal share of false leads and false suspects; in fact, MacLean postpones the resolution of the plot until the last few pages of the book, and the identity of the real villains isn't known until then. His usual stratagem of revealing the mystery about three-quarters of the way through the book has been modified somewhat towards the classic detective story, in which the puzzle is everything, and therefore cannot be revealed until the last moment.

Other characters include the beautiful-but-haughty daughter whom Calvert initially dislikes, but with whom he ultimately falls in love. MacLean obviously has recognized the cliched nature of some of his characters and devices, and has striven to vary the elements in his books by introducing certain exotic settings of unique elements. In *Zebra*, the nuclear submarine gave him an opportunity to expound on something the average reader would not be familiar with; in addition, the possibilities for terror and suspense were increased. Once again, MacLean is following in the footsteps of the classic mystery, which typically features a variety of exotic characters or situations to liven things up for the jaded reader or fan. *Eight Bells* introduces two exotic groups: jet-setters, and a community of Australian shark fishermen living in an isolated village on the Scottish coast. These people are enlisted in Calvert's service to help free the kidnap victims — another familiar MacLean theme — from an old Scottish castle, which they storm in a mad scene that quickly stirs the blood. It's almost as if MacLean had sat down with an encyclopedia and picked out this thing and that, saying to himself, here's something I haven't tried before. The danger of repetitiveness is very real. MacLean is always in jeopardy of writing the same story over and over again. The basic suspense plot involves some kind of secret quest, the submission of the hero and his allies to various kinds of peril, and the resolution of the mystery simultaneously with the safe dominance of the hero. In addition, MacLean uses as his own special trademarks the threat of impersonal climactic forces, and confusion in the identities of heroes, villains and purposes during the course of plot development. But there are only a finite number of variations on these basic themes, and therefore the author must keep striving to present them and rearrange them in such a way that they seem new to the reader, and at least give the semblance of novelty. At times, MacLean is quite successful, making the new developments both interesting and necessary to the plot; in this book, however, the shark fishermen seem rather out-of-place, more forced than logical, more invented for their novelty than really necessary to the development of the story. This aura of sameness about his last three or four novels may have led him to abandon the secret agent/Cold War milieu temporarily, because his next two books are both set in World War II.

Where Eagles Dare (1967) shows that MacLean has learned a great deal about the art of writing in his preceding novels; this book is no simple war story. It combines the war setting with the secret agent milieu, and uses the deceit and duplicity technique that has become one of his familiar trademarks. There are not only double agents, but triple agents and quadruple agents. No one is what he seems. Supposedly, in order to rescue a captured American general who is "the overall coordinator of planning for the exercise known as Operation Overlord – the second front," seven agents are parachutted into alpine Germany to pull him out of Schloss Adler, the "combined headquarters of the German Secret Service and the Gestapo." The originator of the operation is the deputy commander of MI 6, the counter-espionage branch of the British Secret Service. But three of the allied agents sent on this mission are really German spies; the captured general turns out to be an actor sent to impersonate the officer; and Wyatt-Turner, the deputy commander, is actually "the most dangerous spy in Europe, the most successful double agent of all time," for the German side, of course. Only Smith, the leader of the parachutists, is actually what he seems to be, an allied agent attempting to effect the rescue. During the course of the novel, he assumes several different roles and adopts varying relationships with his untrustworthy men; in the end, we find out that his real mission all along has been to entrap Wyatt-Turner, not to free the supposed general-who-is-not-a-general. All of this duplicity is revealed piecemeal in the MacLean fashion; the solution doesn't arrive until the end of the book. The apparent roles of the actors are sketched out at the beginning of the book, and their reality revealed at the end, providing a neat circular plot. The middle section of the novel deals with the infiltration of the castle, and a later attack on its walls, a scene reminiscent of *The Guns of Navarone*, and the assault on its impregnable fortress. In this book, the attack is accomplished more thorugh disguise than outright assault, but the same basic theme is stressed in both.

The primary antagonists in *Eagles* are human, and natural forces play only a minor role. The allied group parachutes into snowy, mountainous terrain, but the setting is used mainly for background affect, and really has little effect on the outcome. Even the primary action scene in the book, where Smith fights his enemies at the top of the aerial tram joining the castle to the village below, is fought mainly on human terms. In war, the major antagonists are men. MacLean has carried his game of hide-and-seek about as far as it can be carried, and still remain explicable. The ploy works in this book: the repeated deceits and the large number of counter-agents build the tension to a high level, with constant twists and turns in the story line. The book is fast-paced, with plenty of action, and little opportunity for the casual reader to think too much about what he's reading.

The revelation of Wyatt-Turner's double game is made in the last few pages of the novel, on the airplane which rescues Smith from the fortress. There is a brief confrontation, which not only proves which of the two is superior, but also demonstrates Smith's awareness of the real game at stake; he's known Wyatt-Turner's identity all along, having disarmed him prior to the denouement. Wyatt-Turner, facing possible execution on his return to England, chooses to step out of the plane and commit suicide, a scene reminiscent of MacLean's earlier novel, *The Satan Bug.* The language of the two books is nearly identical: Scarlatti, in SB, stands in the doorway and looks at Cavel: " 'You never really expected to see me in the old Bailey?' "Cavell replies in the negative, and Scarlatti turns and "steps out into the darkness." At the end of *Eagles*, Wyatt-Turner, having been unmasked by Smith, and learning that his plans have failed, asks: " 'Can you really see me in the tower?' " Smith says no, and so the double-agent leaps to his death. Both scenes are strikingly effective. The lapse may have occurred accidentally; MacLean has written so much that it's quite conceivable he could have unwittingly reproduced the same scene without being aware of the duplication. It also has an additional effect, which MacLean may or may not intend. More often than not, MacLean's villains are more interesting than his heroes, and more complex, pathetic, even more human in many ways. Heroes, after all, tend to be somewhat larger than life, stronger than real men, wiser than the *hoi polloi*, more farseeing than men really can be. Villains have the interesting attributes of evil and malevolence, and also possess a kind of weakness that makes them sympathetic to the reader. Wyatt-Turner is, by every standard, a villainous person; nonetheless, he draws our attention more than Smith, whose very name suggests his bland affability. To use a literary comparison, Iago engages us far more than does Othello.

The last book from this particular period is *Force 10 from Navarone* (1968), which was mentioned earlier in this study. As was noted then, the novel is one of MacLean's weakest efforts, due perhaps to the sequel nature of the book, a very limiting form at best. MacLean seems to have been presented with the idea for a follow-up to his earlier success, and immediately was faced with the problem of what to do with characters whose lives had already run their course. Since their potentialities had already been explored, the survivors of the first *Navarone* epic limped into the second, and just as slowly limped out again. MacLean seems to have learned his lesson from this failure, and has never again tried to resurrect any of his earlier creations. Sequels are rarely as good as the originals; the only exceptions are cycles of novels where the cycle has been planned as a whole; or a particularly imaginative author who is able to build novels one upon another, like layers on a cake, extrapolating each book from the one preceding it. But these are exceptions that just prove the rule.

RENAISSANCE

Following his brief return to the World War II setting, MacLean wrote a series of three novels which seem to have enough similarities and correspondences to be considered together as a group. The first of these novels, *Puppet on a Chain* (1969), is one of MacLean's more intriguing fictions. In many ways, it is the darkest of his books. MacLean has talked of death on many occasions – after all, death is just the other face of fear and suspense – and many lesser characters and villains in his novels have met their share of bad ends. *H.M.S. Ulysses* had several horrifying scenes where characters were torn to pieces, burnt in flaming oil, shot up, drowned, and otherwise killed in the most terrible ways imaginable. But *Puppet*, with its particular rendition of the rituals of dying, and its gruesome emphasis on narcotics, evinces a general tone of unrelieved grimness that is unique in MacLean's canon. The narrator, Major Paul Sherman, head of the London Narcotics Bureau, gives an unappealingly egotistical and smug rendition of the story, with an almost complete lack of feeling. His superhuman feats of daring lift the novel away from what would otherwise be a curtain of total blackness.

For the first time in his work, MacLean makes use of a particular international city to give the novel atmosphere. In this case, the scene is Amsterdam, and the uniquely Dutch features of the setting give the book a most interesting appeal. Until the very end of the novel, the plot seems straightforward and unsurprising. Sherman is searching for some narcotics suppliers with the aid of the Dutch Narcotics Bureau. The criminals are gradually revealed to him and us, without any special surprises, and he avidly pursues them amidst the usual scenes of violence and daring. Sherman is cast in the old traditional image of the amoral agent who works with the law when he can, and outside of the law whenever he feels it necessary. He brushes aside any claims of law and order, and dismisses society's values with a shrug. Nor does he make any claim to national loyalty; the Dutch police are aware of his reputation as a maverick. In short, he's the typical self-righteous individualist, as willing to work for the law as to break it. Another interesting aspect of the book is that Sherman is accompanied to Amsterdam by two young female agents under his charge. In the course of the chase, one of the girls meets a particularly horrible death, pitch-forked by a group of women who surround her and perform a ritual dance. Sherman must look on helplessly. Other deaths in the book include a hanging, broken necks, and extreme forms of violence. Ironically, these horrors seem more vital and understandable than the threats of nuclear missiles, germ warfare, and spy-versus-spy that appear in his other books. When MacLean is dealing with personal matters related by human characters, his novels have a greater sense of reality (and consequent impact) than the socio-political games of the politicians and their agents.

At the end of the book, a surprising twist occurs. Sherman has been supported in his efforts to apprehend the drug dealers by the Dutch police, represented by van Gelder, head of the local narcotics force. Van Gelder's niece, whom he has cared for since the death of her parents, is a former addict; her affliction caused her to stop growing mentally at the age of eight, or so it seems; she is now 23. The personal suffering which van Gelder feels gives him a human and personal aspect lacking in Sherman, and leads credibility to his efforts to track the criminals down; his dedication to the job is understandable on human terms. Then, in a stunning surprise, van Gelder turns out to be the brains of the narcotics operation, and his "imbecile" niece is his mistress and comrade-in-arms. Trudi, the girl, falls to her death in what is, for this book, a typically horrible fashion; after other assorted killings in the final shootout, van Gelder winds up getting impaled on a hook. This last murder is brought about by Sherman, who has an opportunity to capture the crooked cop, but knowing that he may evade prosecution, deliberately kills him. The minions of the law are as violent and ruthless as the criminals. MacLean seems to be saying that perhaps they have to be. And although Sherman certainly has ample justification for his acts in the context of the novel, including various murders of his fellow agents, his complete disregard for due process, the agencies of the courts, and for the concept of the law in general, leaves one with a strangely bitter taste at the end of the book. Neither Sherman nor the reader gets much satisfaction out of the conclusion. When Sherman's amorality is fused with the obscene violence so prevalent in this novel, *Puppet on a Chain* stands out as a unique addition to MacLean's corpus of work.

In contrast to the extreme emotional catharsis of *Puppet*, *Caravan to Vaccares*, MacLean's next novel (1970), is strangely flat and barren. And the flat tone of the novel is matched by an emptiness of plot and style. The book is set in southern France, and deals with a caravan of Gypsies, some of whom are working for various foreign agents. Into this morass is sent Neil Bowman, a secret service agent, who is trying to rescue a kidnapped missile scientist. This justification almost seems in a way to have been thrown in as an afterthought, and is seldom very central to the proceedings. The novel is saved from total failure by a fine opening scene, a prologue, where the Gypsies track and ultimately kill one of their number, an informer, in some prehistoric caves. The murder is described as the ritualistic murder of a tribal member, and the background merely heightens the effect. Also effective is Bowman's guise as a playboy or "layabout." One interesting character, a grotesque duke, turns out in the end to be one of the good guys. But beyond these few bits, the book is curiously talky, very slow-paced, with dialogue that seems more chit-chat than substantial. The suspense is minor, and action minimal. There is an interesting scene where Bowman is sent to his death in a bull ring; his evasion of the animal, whose horns have been honed to razor sharpness, is compelling, although not as well rendered as we have come to expect of MacLean. In the context of the novel as a whole, the bull encounter seems gratuitous and out of pace with the rest of the book. Nothing seems to work very well. It's not that the characters are stereotyped, or that the core of the novel is political ideology, which doesn't seem to lend itself as well to continuous suspense; but merely that MacLean's two devices, the Gypsy caravan and Bowman's disguise, are not enough in themselves to carry a book containing little of anything else. The spark has become very dull indeed.

But if *Caravan* represents a lapse in the canon, MacLean's next book, *Bear Island* (1971), is quite possibly his finest achievement to date. The novel incorporates all the best elements of MacLean's standard themes and motifs. He returns to a first-person narrator, whose ostensible profession is that of a doctor. In reality, of course, he's a secret agent. MacLean seems to enjoy the physician character, having used it previously in several of his more successful novels, including *Night Without End* and *Ice Station Zebra*. And, once again, he returns to the Arctic settings that have done so well for him in the past. The first half of the novel deals with a journey on a boat, another situation MacLean always handles well. All of the elements are present, and they all combine beautifully into an organic whole.

Bear succeeds for other reasons as well, and the book reveals quite clearly how MacLean (and other suspense writers) manages to create dynamic scenes of suspense, tension, and mystery. The conversations and narrations balance each other out: each is just full enough to provide motivation for the characters, and the information necessary to keep the reader strung out, and not so long or rambling as to bore the reader, or make him lose the story line. The mystery is buried beneath a complex, twisting plot. As usual, the opening scene immediately grabs the reader's attention. We are suddenly on board a ship which is "coming apart at the seams" in an Arctic storm. The opening chapter introduces the characters in standard expository fashion. After the initial tensions of the storm have subsided, the Captain tells the passengers that the storm wasn't really that severe, although a number of the people have gotten seasick as a result. All of this is put into focus at the end of the first chapter, when the first death is discovered. MacLean also manages to drop hints that the first body won't be the last. For example, when Dr. Marlowe, the narrator, meets one of the crew members, Smith, he says: "I was beginning to like Smithy though I hardly knew him or anything about him: I was never to get to know him well." The phrase is purposely understated, but provides a suggestiveness from the beginning that death and danger are ranged on all sides, and likely to pursue various members of the crew and the passengers.

Chapter Two retreats from the tensions of the first section; false leads are strewn about, with botulism and salmonella poisoning adduced as the probable cause of death. This rational explanation has been discounted by the end of the section, as Marlowe discovers that the murder was caused by deliberate poisoning, ironically implemented by the innocuous use of horseradish. This is typical MacLean. Fear, jeopardy, terror, death gradually build and come to a point, followed by a logical justification or explanation that places the entire situation into a comprehensible framework. But this rationale is quickly undercut, and the mystery becomes even deeper because of the false leads which have now been discounted. In the third and fourth chapters of the novel, the plot becomes more complicated, and the characters are more fully described. Hints of trouble seem to pop up everywhere on the ship. By the end of the fourth chapter, following several pretended deaths, and two cases of near deaths, the fear and tension increase once again with the confirmation of two more bodies.

At the end of most of his chapters, MacLean tries to introduce some new development into the plot. There may be the discovery of a body, a new twist in the action, an unexpected revelation which will focus the action and move the plot forward onto another level. For example, at the end of Chapter Four, Marlowe returns to his cabin to find that it has been searched in his absence. The mystery of the intruder's identity and purpose deepens the puzzle. In the fifth section, about a hundred pages into the book, MacLean suddenly halts the forward movement of the story, and provides a brief recapitulation of the action thus far, through a discussion of the apparent reasons this particular ship is going with this particular movie crew to this particular isolated Arctic island. The pause allows the reader to catch his breath, before being plunged into the next spate of action, and also gives him a chance to review the situation in his mind. MacLean provides some background information on Bear Island's geography, the history of the movie company, Olympus Productions, and even introduces a map of the isle. All of these details lend an air of credibility to the novel; none are superfluous, since they will all come together into a logical framework at the end of the novel.

After this brief hiatus, Chapter Six moves the plot forward again, with another death, this one a body previously undiscovered. At this point, nearly midway through the book, MacLean allies his central hero, Marlowe, with the man whom Marlowe admired at the beginning of the book, Smith. These two men are the obvious "good guys" of the book. The alliance is an informal one, but it serves to begin the demarcation process that will gradually reveal the solution to the mystery; it also provides us with some background material on Marlowe, whose origins have hitherto been somewhat obscure.

At the beginning of the seventh section, exactly halfway into the novel, we arrive at Bear Island. The journey on the boat occupied the first half of the book; the second part will deal with the island. In Chapter Eight, the boat departs, leaving the movie crew, Dr. Marlowe, and a few others behind; Marlowe and Smith fully reveal themselves to each other, and it becomes clear that they are both agents, although we still do not know whom they are working for, or why. The first bits of revelation come slowly. The ship has come to the island to find some kind of hidden Nazi war loot; one of the movie crew, it seems, is a former S.S. agent who knows what the stuff is, and where it's hidden. We still know very little: many of the characters' roles are yet unclear, and the mystery of the deaths has not been solved.

The action of the second part of the book now begins to parallel that of the first. Deaths begin occurring, and a member of the party is lost – search parties are dispatched to search for him. The same sequential hazards, trials, and deaths turn up in both parts of the novel, and although the comparisons are not exact, the reader now has sufficient knowledge to place these events in their proper context. Chapter Nine, about two-thirds of the way through the novel, advances the plot still further, as new suspects are thrust forward into the action. These suspects are all proved false, and Marlowe summarizes the story to this point in a long speech. This scene is very similar to one common in the detective story, the drawing-room confrontation. The group is all together. The hero goes around the room, listing suspects, motives, suggesting who might be guilty and who might be innocent. In this summary, of course, there is some correct deduction, but also enough incorrect statements so that the mystery is by no means solved.

Further background material is provided in the following chapter, when, for the first time, Smith and Marlowe make their alliance formal, and reveal their true identities. This scene is the private analogy of the public confrontation in Chapter Nine. More tension builds up as the characters are put into increased jeopardy; more suspects come forward, and more suspicious acts are noted. The chapter closes with another thrust ahead: Marlowe discovers the theft of a vial of lethal morphine from his medical kit.

The eleventh and twelfth chapters increase the suspense, which had lapsed during the expository sections of the last two sections. Smith goes off on a fated journey for help, and more men die. MacLean works with a very conventional technique, but makes particularly effective use of it. He brings his action to a peak, and then, usually by exposition or background description, releases the tensions temporarily, only to build them even higher with the next plot twist. This technique is used repeatedly throughout the last chapters. The reader is never quite sure of what is going on until the final denoument. Marlowe and his allies discover the hidden Nazi gold in a tunnel, and their discovery is immediately followed by yet another death.

Chapter Thirteen is the last. In this section, the mystery is finally unravalled. Marlowe reveals his precise identity, that of a British Treasury Agent. In another group confrontation scene, he discusses the gold, and shows who the true villains are. In this particular case, the director of the movie, Otto Gerran, turns out to be the chief instigator of the plot. Several of his fellow movie-makers are also involved, with such matters as blackmail, thievery and murder, but Gerran is clearly the leader, and certainly the most evil. At one point in his career, he apparently murdered his own daughter. In typical MacLean fashion, several twists are tossed in at the last moment. Marlowe reveals Gerran to be the murder, and holds him at gunpoint; suddenly, one of Gerran's people takes over, and their roles are reversed. And then the troops arrive, as Marlowe has planned in advance, and the final shootings and explanations help to tie up the remaining loose ends. The final few pages help relax the reader after his catharsis, and set him gently down with the sense of enjoyment.

MacLean's books work best when he allies evil and the natural forces of violence, when he makes the structure of his novels an undulation of tension, release, and tension, when he manages to twist his plots in such a way as to reveal parts of the mystery bit by bit, until a final stunning denouement at the end. When all these elements mesh together in one harmonious whole, the result is adventure writing at its best. No one understands these things better than MacLean himself, and his popularity is due completely to his total grasp of these techniques. Even his bad books read better than 99% of his competitors' works; at his best, no one else can touch him. His one serious problem has been and will continue to be lack of the right kind of novelty: as time goes on, he has obviously been making a serious effort to diversify his plots, and introduce new and exciting elements that will not give the reader a sense of *deja vu*. Ironically, the further he strays from what he knows, the sea, the Arctic wastes, the narrator-as-observor, the less successful his work has been; all of his best fiction have had one or more of these essential elements. And as we shall see, his latest books all represent attempts to break out of the mold, and all are more or less flawed.

THE SEARCH FOR SOMETHING NEW

After *Bear Island*, MacLean made an obvious attempt to vary his standard formulas by introducing new locales, backgrounds, settings, and even characters. The four novels of this, his most recent period, are substantially different from anything else he has ever written, and are also, for the most part, less successful. There is a certain stiltedness to his recent work that makes it limp, rather than flow, along. In *The Golden Gate*, for example, he is obviously trying very hard to make his characters sound like real Americans; ultimately, however, the book doesn't work: you can research a locale, like the San Francisco setting of the book, but you can't really make it live unless you understand the people. The dialogue is off. The people in the novel stand out quite clearly as the creations of a middle-aged Briton; they neither sound nor act like Americans. This kind of problem turns up in each of the four books published since 1973.

The Way To Dusty Death (1973) is reminiscent of *Caravan to Vaccares*: the dialogue is flat and lifeless, the plot is relatively simple. The book does have some good moments, however, beginning with the action-packed opening. Johnny Harlow, the leading Grand Prix racer in the world, has just crashed in a major race, apparently causing the death of another racer, and crippling the daughter of his car's owner. Harlow turns to drink to assuage his sorrows, and sinks rapidly into dissolution. Soon, however, we learn that everything is not quite what it seems: the deaths are probably not his fault, and Harlow himself is some kind of investigator; he's been using the drunken image to cloak his activities. Harlow gradually begins unearthing the mystery, which, in typical MacLean fashion, is kept hidden until the end. Suspense is minimal: we know that Harlow will triumph over the forces of evil; indeed, he is so effective, so knowledgeable, so much of a superman figure, that it is difficult to imagine anything that might stand in his way.

He can be only temporarily hindered; his ultimate victory is inevitable. Midway through the book, we discover that two major crimes are involved, the fixing of various races on the circuit, and the smuggling of heroin in the transporter which carries the cars around Europe.

Harlowe apparently loves Mary, the girl he is accused of crippling, but his feelings are expressed in such an offhand and ironic fashion that they lend very little to his character. His persona remains curiously bloodless throughout the length of the story. In this book, as in all MacLean novels, sex is virtually nonexistent, and the emotional relationships between men and women are barely hinted at. To MacLean, the most profound human state is the sorrow of a widower grieving for his wife. Beyond that, apparently, one may hold hands, or even exchange a kiss or two with the girl, but never anything else. This absence of a mature emotional development between the two lead characters makes the book seem cold and bare. In the end, Harlow breaks up the heroin ring, rescues the wife of MacAlpine, Mary's father, and destroys the race fixing operation. But good triumphs without the help of the law; although Harlow is connected with either a special branch of Scotland Yard, or with Interpol, he never admits his true relationship to these organizations, and he works outside of established channels. He breaks up the pushers by capturing the suspects, torturing various gang members until they spill the beans; and finally calls the police to mop up the operation after he has disappeared. Harlow admits during the course of the novel that the authorities had broken a number of gangs through illegal activities, using phone taps, surveillances, and the like to crush the criminals with their own means. He seems indifferent to the moral aspects of the situation; he has no regrets or apologies. At the end of the story, one villain remains at large, and Harlowe overtakes him following a high speed chase through southern France. But, rather than take the gangster into custody, the race driver deliberately sends the criminal over a cliff to his death. The implication is clear: the man deserved to die.

In his later fiction, MacLean has turned increasingly to the lone hero fighting against great odds to overcome an organized band of enemies, whether they be criminals, commies, Germans, Indians, or whatever. Most of these supermen have some kind of intangible relationship with the law, but also have an understanding with official forces that they will work on their own outside of normal channels, righting wrongs, and reporting back when they choose. They seek their own forms of justice, their own revenge against the evildoers. The ends justify the means: we must stamp out the insidious forces of crime, Communism, and the Krauts, who peril the survival of civilized man; they can be defeated only by copying their tactics. Vigilante justice is necessary to repair the rents in society's fabric. The judges are soft; citizens must take their places. Johnny Harlow is a particularly amoral representative of this kind of philosophy; the shallowness and callousness in his characterization give *Dusty Death* little in the way of substance.

Breakheart Pass, published in 1974, represents a unique departure for MacLean, his only work to date to be set in an historical framework (if we exclude his novels on the War). The action of the story takes place in the American West during the years following the Civil War, and has all the traditional trappings of the conventional western. Furthermore, MacLean attaches a cast of characters (with tongue-in-cheek descriptions of each) to the front of the book, enhancing its historical nature. For example, Sepp Calhoun is cited as "a villain of some note," two cavalry officers, Capt. Oakland and Lt. Newell, are described as "inactive parts but of considerable relevance to the story." The author also provides a sketch of the various train cars on which most of the story happens, and a map of the fort which is their ultimate destination.

The style is curiously coy and forced, as if MacLean were trying to imitate historical American dialogue, but somehow had no real sense of how his characters should spcak. Sometimes they sound like standard figures from sentimental Victorian fiction; on other occasions, the dialogue is indistinguishable from that in the rest of his work. In fact, the novel could equally well have been set in contemporary England as in nineteenth century America; there is nothing inherent in the plot, subject, or trappings of the novel that require it to be rendered in historical terms, unlike, for example, Michael Crichton's *The Great Train Robbery*, which could only exist in relationship to its insights to Victorian culture and society. All of the standard MacLean conventions are present. The protagonist is a physician, although he is initially presented as a renegade of sorts. Later, of course, we find that he is really "a secret agent of the Federal government." The story follows the journey of a train to rescue the military outpost of Fort Humboldt from a cholera epidemic. The typical MacLean heroine, niece of the Governor of Nevada, manages to fall in love with the hero in the standard emotionless fashion by the end of the book. The Governor and a U.S. marshall turn out to be the crucial villains.

This novel demonstrates MacLean's increasing contempt for society and its trappings, including societal leaders, laws, and civilization in general. The villains in these later books are invariably members of the power structure of the social groups they supposedly represent. The only thing that thwarts their nefarious schemes is the dauntless individual hero working on his own outside of official channels. Corruption, MacLean is saying, is inherent in bureaucratic structures, and the only way it can be cleaned out is by going around it, not through it. MacLean's philosophy has always tended towards right-wing radicalism, which is natural considering the themes of his books. But in the earlier novels, his heroes seemed to work with the officials representing the forces of good; now, it appears, one must go outside the law to accomplish the destruction of evil. Society can only be saved by purging it of the weak, the corrupt, and the stupid. MacLean's obvious contempt for bureaucracy is curious when matched against an equally obvious faith in the man on the white charger, who will somehow right every wrong, and lead society back to its proper course.

The novel begins with the rescue train being sent to Fort Humboldt on its mission of mercy. Ultimately, however, it is revealed that the saviors are really after a storehouse of gold, another old MacLean standby. The corrupt Governor of Nevada, a nefarious marshall, and an army major have agreed among themselves to abscond with the ten million dollars, using the mercy train as a decoy. Deakin, a secret agent, manages to get aboard the train under arrest. Then, he slowly works to overcome the villains, amidst the usual serial rendition of innocent deaths of the helpless people on the train. In a climactic scene at the fort, against what seems to be a superfluous intrusion of Indians and renegade whites, the gold is saved, the fort is restored to order, and Deakin gets the heart of the Governor's niece. If the plot seems overly familiar to readers of MacLean, it still reads well, and is managed in the author's economical and fast-paced prose. Nature is represented only superficially; the major antagonists are human.

Deakin's total control of the situation lessens the suspense that otherwise might be present; once again, we have the feeling that nothing can really go wrong, and good is certain to triumph in the end. Deakin's implacable superiority over everyone else in the book gets monotonous after a while. At one point in the novel, things are going badly for Colonel Claremont, Deakin's main ally: "Claremont shook his head. His spirit seemed to have left him, he was a man close to despair. 'All those murdering Paiutes, heaven knows how many of them, those desperadoes in the coaches behind us, Calhoun and his renegades waiting for us in Fort Humboldt –' 'Don't worry,' Deaking said comfortingly. 'We'll think of something.' Marica looked at him with a coldly appraising eye. 'I'm sure you'll think of something, Mr. Deakin.' 'As a matter of fact, I already have.' " And sure enough, our hero is never at a loss. MacLean's protagonists are so completely in charge in his later books, so confident, so aware of the villains' plans, so resourceful, that they hardly seem human anymore; the loss of their humanity is the loss of the suspense MacLean is trying so hard to achieve. The adventure novel works only when we, the readers, can imagine ourselves in the hero's place, and feel the fear he feels, and understand the dangers of a situation where death is shadowing his footsteps. The author who can make his readers know the feelings of his characters, and recognize them in themselves has succeeded in his craft. The adventure formula requires the triumph of good in the end. But there always must be the possibility of failure to make the triumph seem real to the secret sharer of the suspense. In real life, defeats are as common as victories, and victories are due as often to accidental circumstances as to any resourcefulness of the winner. The writer who fails to take this into account is toying with disaster. *Breakheart Pass*, although written with the usual MacLean competence, is no more than a minor adventure in his canon.

Exotic and unusual surroundings and situations continue to dominate MacLean's next novel, *Circus* (1975), which uses the background ploy of a famous international circus. The protagonist of the novel, Wildermann, is described as a combination aerialist-acrobat-mentalist. Almost literally, the secret agent has become a superman. The plot centers on an attempt made by Wildermann and his circus compatriots to enter a top-secret, heavily guarded Eastern European prison, which maintains a hidden laboratory, and to retrieve from the fortress a scientific formula essential to national security. The novel verges on science fiction in several respects: the formula is supposedly the key to the creation of antimatter; also, MacLean seems to be obsessed with hidden listening devices of every kind, including counter-listening devices, and counter-counter listening devices.

The circus itself is an extraordinary world, peopled with unusual character types, somewhat more eccentric than those MacLean usually deals with. But even the eccentrics verge on stereotype. The hero's allies include such figures as the circus strongman, Kan Dahn; the lasso specialist, Ron Roebuck; and Manuelo, the incomparable knife thrower. Bruno Wildermann is enlisted to obtain the secret information because of his hatred for the communist invaders of his homeland; the prison is located, coincidentally, in his old home town. Wildermann, in addition to being the greatest acrobat in the world, also possesses superhuman strength, a photographic memory, and unusual mental powers which enable him to read other persons' minds. MacLean has created a comic-strip hero; perhaps for the first time in his fiction, all of his characters lack credibility.

Some of the familiar MacLean devices do turn up in this book: for example, he uses the standard boat trip to carry the circus back to Europe. The usual kinds of death and duplicity fill the journey, and the familiar doctor-as-secret-agent is the chief CIA contact for Wildermann. The expected plot twist reveals the doctor to be one of the chief villains in the novel, though his precise motives are left unclear. He may have been working for the Russians, or may just have been a corrupted American selling out for cash; we never really find out. Once the troupe reaches its destination, the action begins to pick up. In a unique twist for MacLean, Bruno falls from the high wire, and apparently dies from a broken neck. Of course, the death is faked, and Wildermann uses the deception to cover his actions at a crucial point in the proceedings. The entrance into Lubylan Prison is comparatively tame, perhaps because MacLean has already pictured Bruno as such an extraordinary fellow that the supposedly hazardous break-in seems almost routine. Once in the prison, Wildermann is confronted by deception and double deception, and faced with several surprise unmaskings; but it is all done in such bloodless fashion that there is little suspense. Bruno is completely in charge, always one step ahead of the game, too aware of what's really happening to generate much interest in what's going on. In one nice touch at the end of the book, Bruno manages to free his family from their prison cells. They all escape rather too easily, the villains meet their fated dooms, and the closing of the novel seems hollow and contrived. In the last line, as Bruno is walking off to marry the girl he met earlier in the book, he is suddenly revealed to be one of the top, and certainly most trusted, agents of the western world.

For the first time, the word ludicrous can be applied to a MacLean novel. Earlier books have contained scenes that stretched the reader's credibility, but they were so marvelously constructed, and so imaginatively handled, that they could be enjoyed for their own sake, without apologies to anyone. In this book, however, the style is so wooden, the plot so contrived, the tone so uncertain (serious or light?), the threats so weak, that we can only come to the conclusion that MacLean had no coherent plan for the novel, and just allowed it to develop willy-nilly, as it would. Rather than the *tour de force* it might have been, *Circus* ranks as one of the worst books MacLean has written thus far, a labored and rather casual effort from a writer whose talents are much greater than this piece of froth would lead us to guess.

The sense of near-burlesque that permeates *Circus* continues in his most recent book, *The Golden Gate*, published in England in February, 1976. The plot is one of his most bizarre. A master criminal attempts to hold hostage the President of the United States, and two visiting royalty from the oil-producing countries of the Middle East. The ambush takes place on the Golden Gate Bridge. The ransom is set at $500,000,000, plus a presidential pardon, and free exit from the country; if the money is not paid by a certain date, the President and his guests will be killed, and the bridge destroyed.

Several interesting gimmicks are introduced in this book. The President is using an exotic motor coach, fitted with a myriad of ultra-modern technological devices; the kidnappers manage to find a duplicate coach, and use it to pull the presidential party into the trap. Branson, the leader of the kidnappers, is a man who is already independently wealthy, with a Ph.D. from a genuine Ivy League school. He apparently is motivated by some kind of cocktail party Freudian hangup against father figures – both the President and the Secretary of the Treasury have become surrogate fathers in his mind, and since he hated his real father, he hates them as well. Branson's colleagues are an interesting collection of odd characters, in the best MacLean fashion. But the action drags badly through the middle part of the novel. After the initial kidnapping scene, there is a long stretch where the kidnappers negotiate with the law enforcement officials surrounding the bridge, and this part of the book moves quite slowly. By setting the scene on the Golden Gate, MacLean has limited the possibilities for action and suspense; the fast movement of a journey, with its attendant opportunities for terror, is completely lacking. In addition, the plot is so far-fetched as to be virtually unbelievable, and believability lies at the heart of giving the reader a sense of fear.

The hero of the book, Revson, is an FBI agent assigned to shadow the President in an undercover capacity. He is described by his superior as "ruthless, arrogant, independent, disliking authority, a loner who consults superior officers only under duress and even then goes hiw own way." Revson is a typical hero of MacLean's late period: ostensibly, he upholds the forces of justice and the law, but actually he asserts his own independence, and does precisely what he thinks best to thwart the insidious forces of evil. He exists primarly for his own willed action, and not for the maintenance of the values and social norms he is sworn to protect. In the course of saving the President and his friends, Revson meets and falls in love with the coyly-named April Wednesday, who is as shallowly drawn as any other MacLean ingenue. Like the heroes described in the author's earlier books, Revson, with all his ruthless ability to draw on, is able singlehandedly to capture or destroy the kidnappers, and rescue the presidential party without any particular effort on his part, and without any real sense of danger that the kidnapping might actually succeed. It's all so easy that we are inclined to wonder why MacLean didn't have the angels coming down to save humanity at the same time, thereby eliminating a lot of verbiage, and the necessity for anyone to actually finish the book.

One noteworthy aspect of the novel is that, because of the straightforward plot-line, and the concentration of the rather sparse action into several different points at start and finish, the book has little of the duplicity we have come to expect in MacLean's fiction. Revson is disguised, to be sure, but the disguise is a very thin one, and he proceeds to overcome the kidnappers by force and violence, not through trickery. He disarms the guards, climbs up and down various parts of the bridge, fools Branson in the usual satisfactory fashion (we wonder at times how such an intelligent and perceptive villain could be so easily deceived into believing Revson is nothing more than a reporter; Branson has planned for everything else: surely he would have thought of this too?), and, in short, goes about the business of saving the President of the United States most efficiently, simultaneously restoring the energy future of the world (the shieks are suitably impressed by this display of American ingenuity), and protecting a national landmark from destruction. Unfortunately, the few moments of action, and the curious and interesting portrayal of Branson's flawed character (intriguing for its flaws), cannot carry the entire book, and the novel is basically weak. The problem of Branson's peculiar psyche is left hanging at the end of the novel, as if MacLean did not know quite what to do with him; the matter is simply dropped. *The Golden Gate* is just another in a string of novels that were better left unwritten.

CONCLUSION

Alistair has obviously reached a crossroads. On the one hand, he remains as popular as ever, selling millions of books annually to a solidly-established audience. Quite clearly, however, his latest efforts are second-rate when compared to *Bear Island* or *Night Without End*, and one wonders whether he will ever regain the magic formula that worked so well in his earlier novels. MacLean seems to have grown weary of the whole game; his last few books lack the imaginative spark that kept his early fiction moving, even when the plots were less than his best. His efforts to diversify his story lines by using settings and characters outside of his direct experience have generally failed. When writing of the sea, the Arctic wastes, and the journeys men make through and over them, MacLean is unrivalled in his ability to generate fear and suspense in his readers. Let us hope he returns to them soon.

BIOGRAPHY and BIBLIOGRAPHY

ALISTAIR MacLEAN was born 1922 in Glasgow, Scotland. During the second World War, he served in the Royal Navy, and later became an English teacher in Glasgow. Following publication of his first novel, *H.M.S. Ulysses*, he devoted himself completely to his writing, and attained his first major success with *The Guns of Navarone*. Fifteen of his novels have since been made into motion pictures, and MacLean is generally regarded as the premier writer of adventure and suspense fiction in the world today. With his second wife, Mary, he lives and works in Haslemere, England.

A list of his published novels follows:

1. *H.M.S. Ulysses*. Collins, London, 1955, 320p, Cloth, Novel
2. *The Guns of Navarone*. Collins, London, 1957, 318p, Cloth, Novel
3. *South by Java Head*. Collins, London, 1958, 320p, Cloth, Novel
4. *The Last Frontier*. Collins, London, 1959, 319p, Cloth, Novel

4A. reprinted as: *The Secret Ways*. Doubleday, Garden City, 1959, 286p, Cloth, Novel

5. *Night Without End*. Collins, London, 1960, 256p, Cloth, Novel
6. as Ian Stuart: *The Dark Crusader*. Collins, London, 1961, 256p, Cloth, Novel

6A. reprinted as: *The Black Shrike*. Charles Scribner's Sons, NY, 1961, 279p, Cloth, Novel

7. *Fear Is the Key*. Collins, London, 1961, 255p, Cloth, Novel

8. as Ian Stuart: *The Show on the Ben.* Ward, Lock, London, 1961, 189p, Cloth, Novel
9. *The Golden Rendezvous.* Collins, London, 1962, 254p, Cloth, Novel
10. as Ian Stuart: *The Satan Bug.* Collins, London, 1962, 256p, Cloth, Novel
11. *Ice Station Zebra.* Collins, London, 1963, 255p, Cloth, Novel
12. *When Eight Bells Toll.* Collins, London, 1966, 255p, Cloth, Novel
13. *Where Eagles Dare.* Collins, London, 1967, 256p, Cloth, Novel
14. *Force 10 from Navarone.* Collins, London, 1968, 254p, Cloth, Novel
15. *Puppet on a Chain.* Collins, London, 1969, 255p, Cloth, Novel
16. *Caravan to Vaccares.* Collins, London, 1970, 251p, Cloth, Novel
17. *Bear Island.* Collins, London, 1971, 286p, Cloth, Novel
18. *The Way to Dusty Death.* Collins, London, 1973, 222p, Cloth, Novel
19. *Breakheart Pass.* Collins, London, 1974, 192p, Cloth, Novel
20. *Circus.* Collins, London, 1974, 224p, Cloth, Novel
21. *The Golden Gate.* Collins, London, 1976, 246p, Cloth, Novel

MacLean has also written three nonfiction biographies: *Lawrence of Arabia, Captain Cook,* and a juvenile study, *All About Lawrence of Arabia.* Most of his books have been published in the United States by Doubleday & Company, Inc., in hardcover, and in paperback by Fawcett Publications.

now available in the Borgo Press series:

Robert A. Heinlein: Stranger in His Own Land,
by George Edgar Slusser B-201

The Beach Boys: Southern California Pastoral,
by Bruce Golden B-202

Alistair MacLean: The Key Is Fear,
by Robert A. Lee B-203

The Attempted Assassination of John F. Kennedy,
by Lucas Webb B-204

The Farthest Shores of Ursula K. Le Guin,
by George Edgar Slusser B-205

forthcoming titles (April 1977):

Up Your Asteroid! A Science Fiction Farce,
by C. Everett Cooper B-206

The Bradbury Chronicles,
by George Edgar Slusser B-207

John D. MacDonald and the Colorful World of Travis McGee,
by Frank D. Campbell, Jr. B-208

Harlan Ellison: Unrepentant Harlequin,
by George Edgar Slusser B-209

just $1.95 at your favorite bookstore

The Borgo Press
P.O. Box 2845
San Bernardino, CA 92406